Everyday Dilemma

Smriti Ranjan

Presentation by *BookLeaf Publishing*

Web: www.bookleafpub.com

E-mail: info@bookleafpub.com

ISBN: 9789358739688

First edition 2023

DEDICATION

To my little brother. To tell him - "Keep Dreaming"

ACKNOWLEDGEMENT

This book would not have been possible without my partner. Thank you for being there throughout this journey always supporting, inspiring and believing in me.

Unhinged

I don't know if I am sad, depressed or dead
inside
Why do I feel this emptiness within
Why is it that there is this loneliness
Why is it exhausting to wake up, exhausting to
move
Why is it tiring to get through the day
No amount of sleep, no amount of coffee, no
amount of sugar
Is able to make me feel better
There is this desperation to make a new friend
And at the same time this fear of being judged,
hurt or left alone
Why is it that I am strolling down the memory
lane so much these days
Why is there this need to be strongly desired
Why is it that I just want to stay in a moment of
past
Why is it that I am feeling so untethered from
the present
Feeling so detached from reality
Living in an unreal dream
Playing with the unleashed fire
Meeting with my anxious insecure self
Why is my self sabotage mode activated

Why do I want to do everything I never wanted
to do
Why do I feel this strong urge to unhinge
Why am I on this path to destruct and destroy
everything I have
Life is going through a phase where everything
hurts
And every moment feels numb at the same time
Nothing good feels good anymore
Even loads of tears are unable to relieve the pain
within
Why is it that I feel so lost, locked inside a big
black box
Why can't I see the way outside
Why am I not able to breathe and still alive
Why do I feel so tormented and so empty at the
same time
Is there a way out of this trench
Is it just a matter of time
Is there a dawn waiting after this night
Is there any light at the end of this tunnel
And will I ever get to see the day again !

Trouble In Paradise

What is love ?
How do you know what is it supposed to feel
like ?
How it should be expressed ?
How it should be felt ?
What is it that matters?
Is it the intentions or
is it the actions ?
Is it about the little things or
is it the big gestures ?
Is it in the words spoken or the words left unsaid
?
Is it something to be found or to be lost into ?
Is it in the smiles shared or the tears shed or the
silence present around ?
Is it a feeling of rushing high or
Is it the sense of calm ?
Is it a shield of protection or
Is it the perfect recipe of harm ?
Is it the sweet dressing on dessert or
Is it the bitter aftertaste of farm ?
Is it the soothing breeze on the shore or
Is it the bright sun that shines upon ?
Is it a feeling everyone should know or
Is it the pain to be protected from ?

Deep inside within my heart

Deep inside within my heart
There was a tiny little scar
What it meant and what it was
Could not be found looking at the stars

A place which has a lot of secrets
Where no one knows what could be found
There I go looking for something
And end up feeling lost and found

You know they say "when you are truly lost"
That's the moment something is found
Sometimes it could be you yourself
Sometimes it's just a transient ground

Whatever it is, feels worth your time
Worth giving a try at least
A treasure hunt in twinkling sparks
A flailing attempt at "the quest within"

Sleepless in Bangalore

Lying in my bed at 3 am in the night
Talking to the moon, discussing my plight
"Why is it so that my nights have become
sleepless?"
Ruining my morning plans, making my days
useless

Everyday I wake up with the promise to sleep on
time
Every night I stay up breaking that promise a
thousand times
It's not like I don't feel bad
Or this vicious pattern doesn't make me sad
But feels like it's beyond my control
To make things right on my own

So I thought why not seek some help
May be someone else can solve this mayhem
But it turns out there are a lot many more
Who had an even higher sleeplessness score
They said.."It's okay..you are not going crazy..
..It's not you..these days are little hazy...."

Then I felt it's not that bad
Perhaps these nights are not that sad

When life was normal..going fast paced..
When I didn't know why I was running in that
frenzy race..
There used to be moments..when I used to wish..
"If only..I could pause for a moment..take some
break..I would have spent a night awake..
Listening to the songs..reading my
books..drawing something stupid..writing my
heart out.."

So may be..it's a blessing in disguise
Things that I wished for..but never did I realise
It feels good to feel good again
Having some time to have a coffee in the rain
Staring at the moon..lost in infinity..
Talking to myself..proving complete insanity....

The Quarantine Time

Have you ever spent so much time with yourself
That you start wondering who you are
One moment a happy kid
Another moment a crazy teenager
Then sometimes an impatient adult
And sometimes a calm senior citizen
Few moments an intense poet
Then there are phases of a cute cartoonist
Moments of a perfect professional
And then comes a phase of feeling completely
lost
Thoughts of who am I ? Where am I going ?
What am I doing ?

Days of complete silence
Nights spent staring at the sky full of stars
Endless playlist of heard unheard songs in
background
Realisation of the utter chaos within
Screaming thoughts of uncertainty
Leaves me bewildered about my own existence

Shea & Shyra

On a lazy Sunday afternoon
Someone came into my life..
Running, jumping, crawling, licking
Making it a paradise..

She wakes you with an innocent brawl
She runs around like an amped up John
She likes to sleep in the bright sunlight
Without putting up a rumpus fight

When she wakes up she has to go
If you miss that, you never know
If you will slip or she will roll
Whatever it would be, be ready for a troll

Whole day she will create a ruckus
Jumping around like a monkey in circus
Smell of food will be an add on
Driving her crazy full on

But
When she looks at you with her cute little eyes
When she comes running with an effervescent
smile
When she jumps around at the sight of food

When she bites everything that she could find
It takes away all your plights
Everything seems simply alright

Maa & Papa

I may no longer be that child who always
Wanted another hug or minute with you
But I still miss you when we are apart

I may no longer need your hand for every step I take
But I still need your acceptance and support for everything I do

I may not be that little child who asked
For all the things I ever wanted in the world
But that's because long ago you taught me
How to go after my dreams

I may no longer be the child who
Looked for you to share every hurt, smile and tear
But I still feel like a child whenever I think of you

I will always love you, maa & papa
With the heart of that little child
Grown only to love you more and more
From deep within my heart

Story Of A Girl

Story of a girl, sitting in her room
Listening to her heart, away from all the gloom
Plethora of emotions, tearing her apart
A new tale of feelings waiting for the start

What's going on her mind
She is yet about to find
Drenched in an ocean of billions of stars
Staring out of window, searching something far

Nudged by few vague thoughts
Memories that she never sought
Why people can afflict her heart
She always thinks in her crippled cart

Inexorable hope and love
Soft and tender like a dove
She is the princess of her dreams
Walking with closed eyes through the streams

But world around is not her place
This is what she feels in solace
Fickle hearts and cynical minds
So profound and easy to find

Every time she expects something
Her hopes are lurched just like anything
Her trust is something meant to be broken
Encumbered with loads of pathetic tokens

Scattered pieces of her aspirations
Born out of sheer desperation
Debilitate her progressing steps
To overcome these daily crepes

All she desires is affinity
From someone and for infinity
Stars are plunging from the sky
Moon is squinting from his sty
Asking her to go to sleep
So that her lovely dreams could peep

She is now in a state of stupor
Expecting an angel in her future
This is how her story ends
All she needs is just a friend!

Survival

What is your elixir ?
What is your happy place ?
Who is your guardian angel ?
What gives you comfort ?
What brings you peace ?
What makes you smile ?
What makes you wipe the tears that you shed ?
What makes you forget the stabbing pain that
you felt ?
What are your thoughts when you close your
eyes?
What is it that your heart desires?
What is it that you dream about ?
What is it that keeps you going ?
What is it that breaks you down ?
What is it that helps you stand ?
What are your disappointments ?
What are your hopes for the new day ?
How do you define pleasure ?
How do you define pain ?
How do you feel when you wake up ?
How do you feel when you go to sleep ?
What do you do when you are having a bad day
?
What do you do when you have a good one ?

How do you know you have to keep going ?
How do you know it's time to give up ?
Do you really need to know everything ?
Or is it okay to stay in the unknown ?
Do you really need to hold on ?
Or is it okay to let go ?
Do you really need someone to be with ?
Or is it okay to be alone ?
What exactly is the secret to survival ?
If you know, do let me know….

Loving Someone

Why do we love someone or anyone?
Do we really know it?
Do we even understand it?
Is it something we do for others or for
ourselves?
Is it an act of care & giving or an act of vanity?
Does it make things better or worse?
When we love, do we really love them for who
they are
Or we love what we expect them to be or hoped
they would be?
Isn't love supposed to make you kind and
patient?
Isn't it supposed to heal your wounds?
Aren't you supposed to be there for people you
love
Or just leave when it's tough?
Is it a journey of hope
Or does it just end in utter hopelessness?
Is love something you do
Or is it something you are?
Is it important for your existence
Or is it existence in itself?

How do you think it can be defined best?

The act of love and loving someone

I think it's - An act of acceptance
Where change is the only constant
An act of care
Where hurt is inevitable
An act of patience
Where chaos will be there
An act of vulnerability
Where trust is not a given
An act of support
When you might not have an anchor
An act of a soldier
When war is at the homeland
An act of a smile
When there are tears all around
An act of soothing rain
When the heat of the sun is too strong
An act of persistence
When it feels too tough
An act of choice
When the choice seems too heft
An act of being there
When you have every reason to leave
An act of commitment
When all you see is adversity!

Prisoner

Have you ever felt like a prisoner to your
thoughts?
Well! I have felt it, almost every day
The vibe of my prison though keeps changing
One moment it's a sunny day with bright hopes
and happiness
Next you know it's dark and dingy
With no sliver of light to be found
Some days I wake up in paradise
Some days it's worse than hell
Some days it's a promised land
Some days it's a land of nothing

When the days are sunny in this prison
The promise of life feels strong
But when the landscape changes around
Everything just feels so wrong

From the high tides of hope
To the flat waves of nothingness
There is cell with every feeling
In this huge prison of consciousness

But who is the owner of this place
Deciding where I spend my days

Is it me or someone else
Holding the map of this space

There are days when I feel in control
Navigating the maze effectively
Pretty close to breaking free
But then I hear a voice behind
Which pulls me back to the darkest rind
Putting me into the strongest binds
Taking away all my strength
Shutting all the doors
Keeping me confined….!!

A 1000 Piece Puzzle

One random morning decided
To buy a 1000 piece puzzle
With a simple thought of finding a way
To improve focus
To do something productive
To get out of my head
And be present in the present
To spend some time together
Without the fights and the arguments
To find the pieces that fit together
To complete the picture
To find what was lost looking at a single piece
To find a way to look at the bigger picture
To learn the importance of every single piece in
the view
To recognise the effort and patience required
For completing the task at hand
To become aware of the importance of every
piece put together
To acknowledge the progress made each day
To realise the time it takes to build something
worthwhile
To feel the anxiety of losing a piece
To experience the fear of the picture being
incomplete

To go through the regret of not being careful
enough
To undergo the pain of looking at the incomplete
picture
To move on to finding ways to complete it
To explore every possible idea to create the
piece which was lost
To work hard enough to make that piece a reality
To understand "Rome wasn't built in a day"
And losing a piece is not the end
There is always a new picture to be imagined
A new reality to be built
A new world to be found and created!!

Home

What place do you call home ?
The place you were born at
Or the place where you grew up
The place your parents live
Or the place you built for yourself
The place where you met your first friend
Or the place where you lost one
The place where you got the best food
Or the place which satiated you hunger
The place with drizzling rain
Or the place with the snowfall
The place with awesome music
Or the place with best books
The place where you were loved
Or the place where you were allowed to love
The place with all the discipline
Or the place with all the freedom
The place which is a sweet dream
Or the place which is a nightmare
The place you were someone
Or the place you were yourself

Mom

When you look at her,
Who do you see?
The woman who loves you,
Takes care of you
Takes care of everyone in the family
Working through every pain and sickness
With a smile on her face
Who knows everyone's likes and dislikes
Who stays up all night when you fall sick
Making your favourite food is always her
priority
Protecting you from Dad's anger
Is her part-time job
Scolding you the worst
When she feels something is wrong
Praying for your health, happiness and success
Despite the sufferings in her life
Thinking about everyone else
Before her own desires
Constantly working to be an epitome of sacrifice
Striving for everyone's love and respect

Or do you see a woman,
Married very early in her life
Given the responsibilities of a wife,

A daughter-in-law and a mother
Without even being asked once
If that is what she really wants
An 18 year old girl had to leave her home
Her parents, her siblings, her friends even her
surname
One destined day everything changed for her
From a loved, spoiled kid she became a woman
Transported to an alien world
Where every face was a stranger
Every name was unheard
Every feeling was unknown
Rules of living in this world
Were different from what she had known
She had some preparation
But mostly she was on her own
Struggling every day every moment from here
on
Trying to be perfect in every role head on
She never really questioned any rule of this
world
Just followed the instructions which were being
told
Over the years of survival
She lost herself to be never found
A woman with no identity of her own
She lived her life only for others
Breathing and moving for everyone's validation
She never got the chance to meet herself

To know herself even for a moment
To be herself even for a moment
She lost the girl running freely through the fields
Laughing and smiling at her stupidities
I wish that girl could be set free
From the strange hold of this society
Where the only one she needs is herself
Loving and embracing every imperfection
Knowing her true identity
Outside the walls of this stupid world!

Paradise

Entered a new world as a 10 year old
Walking through the aisles
Surrounded by lots of dust and rustic smell
Felt an instant connection to this place
As if this kid found a new home
A home where she was meeting new people
everyday
From different eras and location
With lots of love and fascination
Every person she met had a story to tell
Some were real, some were imagination
Despite the truthfulness of the story
Every word had its own gratification

One day this place was an 80s home
With women striving for their rights
Next day it was a fantasy land
With wizards and dragons all over the place
Then some days there were some recognised
people
Telling the stories of their life
Few days hosted some maths geniuses
Solving some biggest equations this world has
known
Some days there was love in the air

Some days were filled with magic
Some days held place for people's pain
Some days were simply ecstatic

Sometimes there was a nothingness
Everyone just chilled in their own spaces
Then again out of nowhere
You can hear the whispers and the laughter
There is something special about this place
No matter which door you knock on
You will be welcomed with open arms
No criticism, no judgment, no condemnation
Only love, acceptance and recognition
It is a safe space for everyone
To express their deepest emotions
Where you can be anything you want
As stupid or as wise
In this paradise!

Lost Words

27

Been so long since I wrote anything
Always trying and failing again
Took a note of things I want to write
But felt so lost without any gain
Even when you want to say so much
You are at a loss of words
What to do with all these feelings
And how to find an outlet for these
All this pain, all this anguish, all this hurt
Choking my throat from within
Always waiting to flow as tears
Needs to be expressed somehow
Or it will eat me up

Getting to know myself

My first ever steps towards myself
Trying to get to know myself
I don't know if it will help
But it is something to try and delve
Getting used to noises outside
Getting to know better the chaos inside
The more time I spend with myself
The more there is a truth to unhide
The voices I have been drowning in noise
I think it's time to hear them right
What is it they want to say
Might lead the way to deeper insights
About the questions I have always had
Paving the way for a better life!

Blues

Hey! Are you awake?
Asked my brain at 10 in the morning
"I am not so sure"
I am awake but don't want to wake up
I am sleeping but not asleep
I want to do a million things today
But not able to do even "One"
I want to go out for a walk
But not able to get to my shoes
I want to eat healthy
But can't stop binging on snacks
I want to read so many books
But can't seem to turn off the screen
I want to write
But can't seem to find the right words
I am surrounded by people
But still feel alone
I want to feel the sun
But am unable to move the curtains aside
I want to feel the hope
But hopelessness has made a permanent booking
in my heart
I want to be alive
But want to cease existing
I want to feel something
But I keep myself sedated with the blue screen

Coffee and Conversations

There is a formula which makes me happy
Which keeps me going when feeling low
The rich aroma of a brewing cup
The bitter flavour of the beans within

From the vibe of the place
To the feel of the cup
From the music in the back
To the people on the front
From the paintings on the wall
To the crockery on sale
From the conversations going on
To the silence around
There is a magic in the air
Waiting to happen in a moment found

There is a certain calm in the chaos
There is a certain feel in the air around
So many conversations brewing on each table
A smile or a tear in every corner

Someone is working alone
Someone is discussing a business idea
Someone is there to just chill and read
Someone is falling in love over coffee

Someone is going through a heartbreak
Someone is working on their dreams
Someone is trying to find their dreams
Someone is trying to change the world
Someone is trying to fit right in
Someone is trying to do a lot
Someone is trying to just get through the day

A lot seems to happen over a cup of coffee
Endless conversations flowing freely

Rain

With my eyes closed and hair unfurled
I walked out on the porch
Feeling tiny droplets on my forehead
And a gentle breeze at the gorge

It felt as if the world stood still
Bewitched at the lovely stance
As the sky poured down with an invigorating
thrill
Making everything break into a dance

The earthy aroma of the soil
The thrumming sound of the water
With a soothing breeze around
Catering to thoughts so confound

Reading "The Pleasures of the Damned"
Poetry with no harm
With a hot cup of coffee
To keep myself warm

Wednesday Morning

Woke up happy after a long time
Not sure why
May be it was a good conversation
May be it was a good night's sleep
May be it was the home made food
May be it was the morning sun
May be it was the special maggi
May be it was the iced coffee
May be it was the idea of a stress free day
May be it was the anticipation of the next movie
May be it was the call with dad
May be it was the hope of next job
May be it was the feel of freedom
May be it was the excitement of finding a
purpose
May be it was the little bit morning stretching
May be it was the 5 minute meditation
May be it was the call from a friend
May be it was the shift in outlook
May be it was the feeling of being okay
May be it was the thrill of starting something
new
May be it was the sigh of ending a bad month
May be it was the completion of this book

May be it was the courage of making a
difference
May be it was the quest of peace
May be it was the sense of calm
May be it was the soothing sound of rain
May be it was the rainbow after the rain
May be it was the taste of blueberry muffins
May be it was the satiated craving of acceptance
May be it was the realisation of hurt
May be it was the starting of healing
May be it was none of it
Or may be it is all of it
No matter what exactly led to this
I am grateful for a morning like this!